Hey, welcome to Bali! Around three million visitors arrive in Bali each year, and no wonder!

There's crystal clear water to snorkel and swim in, white sand beaches to laze on, majestic volcanoes to climb and bike down, rushing rivers to raft on, and forests full of naughty monkeys to explore. And that's not all: whether you want heart-stopping thrills, to see animals up close, try out your artistic skills, or just eat yummy food – there's plenty to do and see!

So, what are you waiting for? Follow your guide dog, Go!

kids*Go!* Travel Guides
Written by Mio Debnam
Illustrated by Tania Willis

Design Director: Timothy Jones /Designer: Katie Kwan
Published by Haven Books Limited, Hong Kong
ISBN 978-988-18967-9-7
Copyright © 2011 by Haven Books Limited
www.havenbooksonline.com

NOTE TO OUR READERS: We try to recommend the best
attractions, restaurants and tour providers, using trusted
word-of-mouth recommendations; however, we cannot be held
responsible for the safety, scope and quality of their service.
We also strive to provide the most accurate information
possible, but of course, some things may have changed by
the time you visit. If you do notice anything inaccurate in our
guide, or think we've missed out on listing something really
good, please help us to make it better by letting us know about
it. We'd also love to hear from you about all the things you
liked or disliked during your trip, so we can continue to keep
our guides as up-to-date and reliable as possible. How to tell
us? Simply log on to the Family Feedback page at:

www.kidsgotravelguides.com

CONTENTS

SLIDE, SCREAM AND SPLASH AT WATERBOM BALI

Jl Kartika Plaza, Tuban, Kuta
Tel: 0361-755-676

Your whole family will have a blast at this waterpark! You can swoosh down towering slides; take a swim in various pools; have a relaxing ride on the Lazy River; or even get a massage. Some of the big slides have height restrictions (you have to be over 100cm/3 feet 3 inches, and for some, 120cm/4 feet) – but don't worry if you're too short to go on them because there's Bombastic, a fun kids-only area (maximum height 120cm/4 feet) that has enough slides, twisting rides, shallow pools and water cannons to keep anyone busy and happy! Out of the water, there are restaurants, shops, a climbing wall, a bungee trampoline, and a place where you can get a funky temporary tattoo. Open every day from 9am–6pm except on Hari Raya Nyepi – the Balinese Day of Silence (see pg 47).

STEP BACK IN TIME: VISIT AN ANCIENT BALINESE VILLAGE

Tenganan Village (eastern Bali, near Candidasa)

Get a glimpse into the past at this centuries-old walled village. The villagers might prize their cell phones as much as we do but, in many ways, the Bali Aga people still live as their ancestors did several hundreds of years ago. Wander down the street and it's likely you will be invited into the small buildings that line the street. Many of the villagers are craftsmen, and often the front of their house is their workshop. You'll be able to watch them creating finely woven basket-ware, pottery and musical instruments, as well as the special fabric – called the *geringsing* (or 'double weave *ikat*') – which Tenganan is famous for. Cars and motorcycles are banned in the village, but watch out: the occasional buffalo, might be wandering down the road! The villagers dress modestly here, so when you visit, remember not to wear shorts or clothes that expose your shoulders.

A WILD ANIMAL ENCOUNTER AT THE BALI SAFARI AND MARINE PARK

Jl Bypass Prof. Dr. Ida Bagus Mantra, Km 19.8, Gianyar
Tel: 0361-950-000

Beat the crowds by arriving when the park opens – at 9am on weekdays, and 8.30am during weekends and public holidays! First take a ride through the wild animal enclosure – past all sorts of animals such as zebras, cheetahs, and hippos; then visit the komodo dragon, white tiger and elephant enclosures. You can even pet some hand-reared wild animals (apparently, the tiger cubs and orangutans are sleepy because they've just been fed – we hope that's the case). Afterwards, watch some animal shows or take a look at the fish in the aquarium. If that's not enough, you can watch, and try, some Balinese dancing, go to the Fun Zone to cool off in the swimming pools, or go on a ride in the mini theme-park area. If one day isn't long enough to do everything, maybe your parents would consider staying a night next door at the **Mara River Safari Lodge** (tel: 0361-747-5000), where you can go to sleep listening to the big cats roaring. Call for details on different packages available, shuttle bus service etc. Park closes at 5pm.

* Note on addresses: Jl = Jalan = Road

VISIT UBUD!

Escape the heat of the beach resort for a night or so and travel to the lush green hills of Ubud. There's something for everyone – you'll be able to watch performances of **traditional dance and music** (pg 8/10), learn how to dance yourself or try out some other **arts and crafts** (pg 30/31). Take a walk through the **monkey forest** (pg 21), **ride a buggy** (pg 28), go **white water rafting** (pg 25), have an action-packed day at **Green Camp** (pg 26), or visit ancient **temples and caves** (pg 14/15). You can also ride an elephant at the **Taro Elephant Safari Park** (pg 16), or visit the **Bali Bird Park** (pg 19) and the **Rimba Reptile Park** next door (pg 20). When you're done with all that, enjoy the shops (pg 34/35) and the nice food (pg 42/43) that Ubud has to offer!

GLIDE THROUGH THE AIR AT THE BALI TREETOP ADVENTURE PARK

Bedugul Botanical Gardens, Candikuning
Tel: 0361-852-0680

High on a hill in the Bedugul Botanical Gardens, an exciting treetop adventure awaits! Anyone over 95cm/3 feet 1 inch tall (approx 4 years old) is welcome to test his or her agility and nerve

at this park, which is open daily from 8.30am–6pm. The park prides itself on its safety standards, and the instructors make sure you know how your equipment works, and that you can make it around the practice circuit, before they set you loose. Clip on your safety line and then you'll be off – swinging, ziplining, and swaying on aerial walkways high in the treetops! There are six different courses – with the easiest two being for kids aged 4–8. The hardest course is only open to those over 140cm/4 feet 7 inches tall or over 12 years old. We'd recommend buying the reasonably priced fingerless gloves they have on sale there.

If you visit close to lunchtime, bring a picnic, or stop at a café in nearby Candikuning. Afterwards, if you're not too tired, visit **Pura Ulun Danu Bratan** – an interesting temple complex, where you can go boating too (pg 10/11)!

BE A CULTURE

Bali is full of interesting things — serene temples and historic villages (see pg 10/15) and sites, as well as lots of traditional arts, crafts, and cultural performances. If you become inspired, you can even learn how to dance, or create an artistic souvenir (see pg 30/31).

SHOW TIME!

Shadow puppet show

Known as the Wayang Kulit, shadow puppet shows are performed all over Bali – before ceremonies, during festival times, or just for fun. The *dalang* (the storyteller and puppeteer) tells a traditional tale featuring lots of different puppets. Often he'll include village gossip and comedy in the show too, to keep the audience laughing. A village show might last from evening till dawn, but shows designed for tourists are a lot shorter. Weekly shows are held in **Oka Kartini** (tel: 0361-975-193, see Ubud map, pg 54), as well as in **Banjar Buni** (Jl Raya, Kuta, no telephone). Ask your hotel for more details.

Traditional dance

Hold on boys – don't skip this section! Balinese dance is not just for the girls, and no visit to the island is complete without seeing a traditional dance. We'd recommend the Barong or the Kecak Dance for color and excitement, and the Legong dance if you want to see some graceful moves. Read on for more details!

The Barong Dance

This dance is about the battle between good and evil. In it, Bali's guardian and the king of the spirits, Barong – a large scary mythical creature with a red face and elaborate headdress – fights with the demon queen Rangda, who has a white face surrounded by shaggy hair.

VULTURE

Many hotels have dinner shows featuring short dance performances. You can also go to watch public performances, particularly around Ubud, Denpasar and Kuta. Be warned though, a full performance goes on for a few hours! If you're in Ubud, ask about times and venues at the Tourist Office – called the Yayasan Bina Wisata (Jl Raya Ubud, tel: 0361-973 285, see Ubud map on pg 54).

Accompanied by hypnotic *gamelan* music (see pg 11), the dance has action and an exciting storyline! It also features graceful dances by female dancers as well as some *kris* (sword) dances by the men.

The Kecak Dance

This is one of the most unusual dances performed in Bali – why? Because there is no *gamelan* music and no colorful costumes. Instead, the music and action are produced mainly by a choir of about a hundred men,

BE A CULTURE

who represent the monkey army. It's their constant battle chant of 'KEK' which helps Rama defeat the evil Ravana. You'll find your pulse racing as you listen to the chants and watch the action! (see pg 12)

The Legong Dance
You'll be surprised at the youth of the Legong dancers – traditionally, the dancers are as young as 8 years old. You'll also be blown away at their grace, as they move fluidly to the music of the *gamelan* orchestra.

TONS OF TEMPLES

There are loads of temples (or *pura*) in Bali – many in stunning locations. Tourists are usually not allowed to enter the buildings and some of the inner courtyards, but even so, it would be a shame not to visit at least one *pura* to soak up the atmosphere. If you're lucky, you may even get to see a ceremony!

Pura Ulun Danu Bratan
Jl Pancasari-Baturiti, on the western shore of Danau (Lake) Bratan
Farmers go to this temple to pray for rain, but the tourists pray for good weather so they can take photos of the *meru* (shrine with multi-tiered thatched roofs), standing on an island in the lake. But there's more to

do than snap pics – you can also rent a rowboat or a pedal-boat and leave the crowds behind. If you're a reptile lover, pay a visit to the temple snake before you leave. Afterwards, head towards the nearby village of **Candikuning** to enjoy a sweet treat made with locally grown strawberries (when they're in season). If you're still bursting with energy, take your family to the **Bali Treetop Adventure Park** (pg 6/7), where you can fly among the treetops! Note: don't confuse the Bratan temple with the similarly named Pura Ulun Danu Batur, which is located farther east, on the edge of a volcanic crater overlooking Lake Batur.

Did you know?

The magical, rhythmic music that is so characteristic of Bali is made by a gamelan – an orchestra of Balinese flutes, drums (which are played using the hands), bronze gongs, and various bronze and bamboo instruments – which are played using small hammers.

Pura Goa Lawah
Jl Raya Goa Lawah, near Kusamba, east Bali
You probably wouldn't encounter this temple unless you were on the way to Kusamba (to see how salt is made), or to Candidasa. However, if you are nearby, you should definitely visit this ancient site – people have been worshipping there for about 1,000 years. The shrines are small, but the holy cave in the cliff face is amazing. It's home to thousands of bats – and quite a few pythons too. Legend says that a tunnel from the cave leads

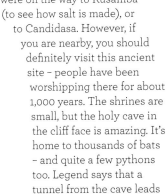

BE A CULTURE

to another temple miles away; but when you get a whiff of the bat poo, we guarantee you won't be volunteering to investigate!

Pura Tirta Empul (Temple of the Holy Water)
Jl Tirta, north of Tampaksiring, near Ubud

The beautiful Tirta Empul temple was built nearly 1,100 years ago, around a sacred spring. Within the inner courtyard of this temple, the Balinese make offerings, pray, feed the *koi* carp and take a dip in the crystal-clear water. The water of the spring is said to help cure illnesses, so you often see people collecting it in bottles to take home. Come early in the morning if you can, to beat the tour buses.

Pura Luhur Uluwatu
Jl Uluwatu, southwest tip of the Bukit peninsula

This temple – one of the oldest in Bali – is on the southwestern tip of Bali. The views from its steep cliff-side location are fantastic, but you won't be able to enter the temple itself. If you visit at sunset, you might be able to catch a performance of the Kecak dance, but beware as it's often very crowded then, with lots of hawkers (people who try and sell you stuff) pushing and shoving. Also, the monkeys that live at the temple are very, very cheeky. Make sure that all jewelry, cameras and anything bright or shiny are out of sight, or you might lose them to a quick-fingered macaque. They particularly like stealing hats, glasses and sunglasses, so it's worth tucking them away in a bag. Don't say you haven't been warned!

Pura Tanah Lot (Sunset Temple)
Jl Raya Tanah Lot, Tabanan

This temple, built on a rock in the sea near Canggu, is one of the most popular tourist sites in Bali. However, a large portion of the rock it stands on is artificial (the natural stone got worn away by the waves, and had to be restored); foreign visitors cannot enter the temple building; and like its sister temple Uluwatu, it is often overrun with a noisy crowd of hawkers. So why is it

VULTURE

still so popular? The Balinese go there because it's an important religious site. The tourists go there to photograph the 'temple on a rock', because it is an amazing sight! It's most dramatic at sunset, but that's when it's most crowded, so if you really want to go we'd recommend you head there in the morning. Oh, and don't forget to pop into the little temple building on the beach, to meet the huge snake that lives there.

If you plan to visit any temples or holy sites, you'll need to wear a sarong around your waist and legs, and cover up your shoulders. You may be able to rent a sarong, but just to be sure (and save money!), it's a good idea to tuck one into your bag before you go.

BE A CULTURE

Pura Petitenget
(Temple of the Secret Box)
Jl Kayu Aya, Seminyak

Petitenget is a directional temple, which is often used for ceremonies. There are many legends about how the temple got its odd nickname. One tells of a holy man from Java who visited Bali centuries ago. It's said that he left a mysterious box when he departed. The locals, out of respect for the monk, never opened the box; but because they believed it was holy, they built a temple around it. The good thing about this temple is that it's usually not crowded! If you're there on Sunday, go for brunch at **La Lucciola** (pg 36) afterwards.

GIANT'S NAIL ART AND OTHER ROCK CARVINGS

Gunung Kawi
Signposted from the northern edge of Tampaksiring village, near Ubud

Buy a drink, or two, before you start walking down the narrow set of steps leading to Gunung Kawi – they are steep, and there are a lot of them! Along the way you'll see lovely rice-paddy views, and by the time you reach the valley, you'll feel like you've been transported back in time. Walk along the valley floor to examine the 1,000 year old *candi* (shrines), which have been carved into the rock face. If you step back and look at the shape of the 10 *candi*, you'll see why some people think that Kebo Iwa (a Balinese folktale giant) dug the shrines out of the rock with

his fingernails! Historians believe that they were built to honor people in the royal family, with the five largest (they're about 8 meters/26 feet tall!) being for the most important members. Unlike many other attractions, Gunung Kawi tends to be fairly deserted. The walk and the steps put people off, so it's peaceful!

Goa Gajah (Elephant Cave)
Jl Raya Goa Gajah, Bedulu, near Ubud
There were no elephants in Bali when this cave was dug out from the rock face 900 years ago (legend has it that Kebo Iwa was responsible for this one too!), but the rather scary face carved above the entrance looks somewhat like an elephant. It is, however, more likely to be a demon or Rangda the witch. Enter through the mouth of the demon, and you'll find yourself in the tiny cave, along with some statues – one of which is of Ganesha, the elephant-headed Hindu god. Outside are a couple of small pools of holy water where the Balinese can bathe. Sadly, visitors are not allowed to join in. Try to get here before 10am, when the tour buses arrive.

Yeh Pulu (ancient carvings)
Off Jl Raya Semebaung, southeast of Goa Gajah, Bedulu, near Ubud
Yeh Pulu is not as old as Gunung Kawi and Goa Gajah – being only about 700 years old – so it's not on the tourist trail. However, the lovely green setting and 25 meters/82 feet of carvings on the rock wall make it worth stopping by, especially if you're visiting Goa Gajah, which is only a few minutes away by car. The carvings show how the ancient Balinese lived – there are pictures of day to day life, as well as a few hunting scenes. Some of the carvings also show scenes from Balinese myths.

HAVE A WILD RIDE!

Taro Elephant Safari Park
Jl Elephant Park Taro, near Ubud
Tel: 0361-721-480

This huge, green park is home to about 30 Sumatran elephants – many of which used to be work elephants – and their naughty babies. You can feed and stroke them, and learn all about them from the knowledgeable *mahouts* (keepers) who look after them. Watch the elephant talent show, and then clamber onboard to have a ride through the forest! If that isn't enough 'elephant time' for you, consider spending the night at the **Elephant Safari Park Lodge** (call 0361-721-480 to book) which is part of the park. Guests at the hotel are picked up by an 'elephant-chauffeur' and taken on treks or to dinner; and they also have the opportunity to help with the elephant's bath, if they wish! The **Bali Adventure Tours** company, which owns the park, can also arrange other activities such as white water rafting, kayaking, trekking etc (pg 25). Warning: there are several other similar-looking elephant parks – some of which do not look after the animals as well as they do at Taro. To make sure you visit the right park/hotel, book via Bali Adventure Tours, at the number above.

Bali Camel Safari
at the Hotel Nikko, Jl Raya Nusa Dua Selatan, Nusa Dua
Tel: 0361-776-755/ 081-236-79336

Sway along the sand on a 'ship of the desert'! The Bali Camel Company, based in the Hotel Nikko grounds, offers 'safaris'

ANIMALS

– otherwise known as a ride along the beach! – on a troupe of gentle dromedaries (single-humped camels). Each camel can carry two passengers. You can choose just to have a camel ride (for either 30 minutes or 1 hour), or combine it with a trip to Turtle Island, where you will be able to parasail, banana boat or ride in a glass-bottomed boat. Call for more details.

HORSE RIDING

If you've already had a ride on an elephant or camel and would prefer to explore on the back of a horse or pony, try one of the two stables below:

Umalas Horse Stables
Jl Lestari 9x, Banjar Umalas Kauh, Kerobokan
Tel: 0361-731-402

This well-run stable not only offers lessons and pony rides, they also run sightseeing 'tours' on horseback – from gentle half-hour walks through peaceful rice paddies and villages; to 2 or 3 hour rides to the beach via the village and rice paddies. Beginners and kids are well looked after – each will be given their own personal guide to make sure they are safe and happy. Hard hats and chaps (leg protectors) are provided, but it's recommended that you wear a pair of shoes with a small heel. Horse-crazy families can stay in the lovely little boutique hotel next door (with a pool and adventure playground for the kids, as well as a nice restaurant and spa treatments for your parents), and take advantage of the ride/stay packages. Call for more details.

Kuda P Stables
Gang Sabana 6a, Banjar Kang Kang, Pererenan. Tel: 081-238-39731

Like the Umalas Stables above, the Kuda P offers a variety of enjoyable horseback 'tours' off the beaten track, through the Balinese countryside. The tours range from half an hour (most suitable for beginners or the very young – they have docile ponies for kids aged 4+), to two hours for those who would like to see both rice paddies and the beach! Hard hats and chaps are provided, and they can arrange for you to be picked up from your hotel too. Call the number above for more details. If possible, wear a pair of shoes with a small heel.

WILD ANIMALS

Bali Turtle Conservation and Education Center
Serangan Island (Turtle Island), near Sanur
Tel: 0813-3841-2716
In the past, Bali was bad news for turtles: tens of thousands were killed each year as their flesh is considered a delicacy. Luckily, they are now protected by law, and turtle hatcheries like those on Serangan Island have helped too. You can drive to Serangan Island, which is also known as Turtle Island, or choose to visit it by boat from Tanjung Benoa. Book a tour or call ahead of time to make sure the center is open to visitors. If you're very lucky, you might get the chance to release a baby turtle into the sea!

Dolphin-watching trip
From Tanjung Benoa
The best place to see the dolphins is off the coast of Nusa Dua – several of the water-sports companies organize dolphin-watching trips from Tanjung Benoa (see pg 22). Trips can be arranged at most times of the day, but you are more likely to see dolphins early in the morning and at sunset. There are no guarantees

ANIMALS

you will see any at all, but most visitors do manage to see a pod (group) of dolphins, racing and leaping in the ocean. A more landlocked location to see them is in the dolphin pool of the **Melka Excelsior Hotel** (tel: 036-241-562) in Lovina, north Bali. The hotel's 'swim with dolphins' experience is popular, but we hope you'll choose to see dolphins swimming freely in the ocean rather than those in a pool.

Bali Bird Park & Rimba Reptile Park
Jl Serma Cok Ngurah Gambir, Singapadu, Batubulan
Bird Park, tel: 0361-299-352. Open 9am–5.30pm
Reptile Park, tel: 0361-299-344. Open 9am–6pm
If you can't decide which park to visit, consider buying a combined ticket and visiting both – they're next to each other! The bird park is quite big – and care has been taken to try to recreate the natural habitats of the birds from different parts of the world. You'll feel as if you are in the jungle as you wander through the aviaries – one of which has a walkway up in the treetops! The park is home to about 1,000 birds of 250 species, from the jewel-colored birds of paradise, to the fierce serpent eagles, to the giant flightless Cassowaries. Go early, as it is sometimes possible to feed the birds at 9.30am.

TALK TO THE

The reptile park is a bit smaller but it's also set in a lush green garden. As you walk along the twisting paths and past waterfalls, you will be struck by the variety of animal 'song' that you can hear. Most of the nearly 200 reptiles are housed in glass-fronted displays – which you'll be glad of, when you see how many poisonous snakes and sharp-toothed crocs and lizards they have. Those who want to get up close and personal can get a photo taken with a friendly python or an iguana. Make sure you don't miss seeing the giant Komodo Dragon – but don't get too close, as it can be dangerous!

Bali Safari and Marine Park

Larger, and with a better reputation for looking after their animals than Bali Zoo. Here you can spend the whole day exploring all the different parts of this park. Read more on pg 5.

MONKEY WATCHING

Sangeh Village Monkey Forest

**Sangeh Village,
Central Bali,
to the west of Ubud**

The Balinese believe that macaque monkeys are the descendants of the Hindu Monkey King, Hanuman, so in the nutmeg forest near Sangeh Village they are treated royally and

ANIMALS

There are many animal attractions in Bali, but some are better than others. Imagine how boring it would be to live in a tiny room with nothing to look at or do. Animals get bored too, so giving them enough space, a natural environment, companionship and things to keep them busy is as important as feeding them, to make sure that they stay healthy. Wild animals also shouldn't be handled too much – some places drug animals to let tourists play with them. If you see an attraction that isn't animal friendly, let us know, so we can warn others not to go – until conditions improve!

allowed to roam freely. They are interesting to watch, but don't get too close – and make sure that things like food, drink, glasses, hats, cameras and jewelry are hidden in a large bag (or left in the car) or you might find that the monkeys come and snatch things right out of your hands. Those who venture to the middle of the forest will find a temple (Pura Bukit Sari) with a large statue of Garuda – a mythical bird-like creature – in the courtyard.

Ubud Monkey Forest
Padangtegal, Ubud
If you're visiting Ubud, the monkey forest is easy to get to – just stroll down Monkey Forest Road. The long-tailed macaques are used to tourists, and are very cheeky as a result. There are bananas for sale, but we'd recommend that you do NOT buy any, or you might be mobbed! Remember, don't take anything interesting-looking and don't get too close. Walking among the monkeys is pretty safe but never forget that they are wild animals – so don't get too playful with them if you don't want to get bitten! If you walk far enough, you'll find a temple at the far end of the forest.

GET WILD &

Waterbom — waterpark

A huge waterpark with awe-inspiring slides that will make you scream! Lots of fun for the whole family. See pg 4 for details.

Tanjung Benoa — water-sports beach

Older kids who like a thrill will enjoy a day at Tanjung Benoa Beach, near Nusa Dua. If you want a peaceful beach experience, however, avoid it as the sea is full of buzzing jetskis and roaring speedboats towing parasailers, banana boaters and flyfish (a blow-up raft/kite that flies up in the air) fans. There are several water-sport companies along the beach. Some are better than others, so ask your hotel to recommend a trustworthy one, which has proper equipment and well-trained staff, and book in advance. Remember to follow instructions and wear all the safety equipment!

Camp Splash

Sanur Paradise Plaza Suites,
Jl By Pass Ngurah Rai 83, Sanur
Tel: 0361-281-781

Camp Splash is an (almost) parent-free zone! Kids can enjoy a day of activities, both outdoors: swimming in the pool, whirling down a waterslide, and playing beach soccer or basketball; and indoors: watching movies/cartoons, playing darts, pool or table tennis or even video-arcade games. You can even get your face painted, or hair braided! The camp is free for people staying at the hotel or apartments, but anyone can

WET

participate for a reasonable fee. Kids younger than 4 must have a parent present, but anyone older can wave 'bye to parents at the door.

GO CRUISING

Have a day on the ocean waves by getting a boat to a nearby island – e.g. to popular Lembongan Island. Once there, you can ride a glass-bottomed boat, go snorkeling, or even do a Marine Walk – where you put on a helmet (which is open at the bottom and connected to an air supply), and take a stroll on the seabed! There are several companies that can arrange cruise tours. One such company is Bali Hai Cruises. Call them at 0361-720-331 for details of different trips.

GO SNORKELING

If you're a confident swimmer, you should try snorkeling! Once you get the hang of it, you'll want to drift for hours watching the fish. It's best to try it out in a pool first, and learn how to 'clear' your snorkel of water, so if a wave slops water down your snorkel pipe, you can deal with it. If you go snorkeling in the sea, make sure you don't become separated from your group! There are many good places to go snorkeling – here are a few suggestions:

- Lembongan Island (see above)

- Menjangan Island (off the northwest coast of Bali) – part of the Bali Barat National Park.

- Gili Islands – the Gilis are several hours away from Bali, by boat. **Warning**: the current can be extremely strong, so only snorkel in the recommended areas.

GET WILD &...

Learn how to ride the waves from an award-winning surfer!

Bali has two excellent surf schools. They hold their lessons in waist-high water so it's pretty safe, but remember, the currents can be strong, so this is recommended for those who are strong swimmers and aged 8 or above. If you're hungry after surfing, grab some food on the roof terrace of **Zanzibar** restaurant (pg 38).

Quiksilver Surf School
Jl Pantai Legian Kaja (next to the Jayakarta Hotel)
Booking Tel: 0361-731-078
This school is run by a world-champion surfer – and all the coaches have been trained by him, so they should all be good! Whether you're a complete beginner or an advanced surfer, they have classes that will help you become even better. They recommend private lessons for younger kids (they must be strong swimmers, and 6 years is the minimum age) but older kids or experienced surfers can join a small class. The first three lessons are in waist-deep water, before you head out a little farther to catch the waves!

Ripcurl School of Surf
Jl Arjuna, Kuta
Tel: 0361-735-858
Kids aged under 12 are given individual attention at the Ripcurl school – there'll be

an instructor for every two kids. All the instructors are good – and trained to international levels, so you'll be able to ride the waves in no time!

INNER ISLAND THRILLS

Visiting Ubud? Go white water rafting down the Ayung River. The voyage takes about an hour and a half , and you'll experience both fun and fear as you swoosh down over 25 rapids. The guides are all very well trained and experienced so you don't have to worry! In between the rapids, sit back and enjoy the scenery. At the end of your ride, you'll be able to shower and have a meal before you go back to your hotel. We recommend you wear lots of waterproof sun-lotion, and a t-shirt over your swimsuit or your shorts. Helmets and life-jackets will be provided. Here are two well-established rafting companies we recommend:

Sobek Bali
Tel: 0361-768-050
This company which specializes in white water rafting (in large rafts which hold several passengers and the guide) and cycling tours has been in business for over 20 years, and has a reputation for safety.

Bali Adventure Tours
Tel: 0361-721-480
You can kayak (with a guide, on a 2-person kayak) or take the larger rafts down the rapids with Bali Adventure Tours. They also arrange bike tours, and hikes that include a visit to the **Taro Elephant Safari Park** (pg 16), which they own and run.

NON-STOP A

There are a lot of fun, heart-pounding activities to do in Bali — such as surfing, rafting and other water activities (pg 22/25), and your heart will definitely be pounding if you visit the Waterbom (pg 4) or the Bali Treetop Adventure Park (pg 6/7)! But that's not all — here are more fun things for you to try:

Green Camp Bali

Green School, Jl Raya Sibang Kaja, Banjar Saren, Abiansemal, Badung. Tel: 0361-469-875

Go to camp in a *school* during your vacation? Well, yes, but this is no ordinary school! It's nestled in a lovely green setting, all the buildings are made of bamboo, they grow their own rice, and the classrooms are open-air. The students who go to the international Green School have the same type of lessons that you do at your school, and take exams and stuff, but Green Camp isn't about books and math … it's about FUN!

There are two programs – a day program for kids aged 5–11 (which involves a lot of messy outdoor fun, exploring the jungle, games, races and interesting art projects), and another for kids aged 12–17. Older kids can also choose to stay overnight for the 'adventure camp', which involves activities such as tubing or rafting down the river, hurtling into the river from a cliff top, rock climbing, blindfold tag in a mud pit, night safari and Amazing Race-style team activities. Green Camp is open 363 days a year – call for details.

CYCLE BALI

Get close to nature, on a bike! There are many options for biking in Bali – most of them involve a fairly easy ride downhill in the cooler mountain air, with plenty of stops scheduled for you to catch your breath, take photos and listen to your guide tell you about your surroundings.

The two tour companies we recommend will pick you up from your hotel, provide your bike and helmet, feed you a yummy buffet lunch at the end, and take you home in air-conditioned comfort! Sports shoes, mosquito repellent and sunscreen, comfortable clothes and a change of clothing (in case you get really sweaty) are recommended.

Sobek Bali
Tel: 0361-768-050
Cycle downhill on the slopes of Mount Batur passing villages and stopping at temples. The company can also arrange a tailor-made tour for you if you call a few days in advance.

Bali Adventure Tours
Tel: 0361-721-480
The standard tour is a 25km/15-mile ride down Mount Batur, and along villages to the Elephant Safari Park at Taro – where free entry is included. Easier or more adventurous cycling tours can also be arranged. Call for more details or to arrange.

NON-STOP A

Bali Buggy Discovery Tour
**Office: Jl Wirasatya Vi, no. 7X,
Suwung Kangin, Denpasar
Tel: 0361-720-766**

The Discovery Tour company will pick you up from your hotel, and take you to the Payangan area, just north of Ubud – about 1.5-2 hours drive from Kuta. Here, the pilot (who has to 16+) and the passenger (who has to be 5+) will be able to practice driving on the training track, before going on a 2-hour guided tour through the countryside. At the end, there will be a chance to clean yourself up – you might be muddy! – before a yummy lunch and the trip home.

Paintball Bali
**Jl Karang Putih 1, Jaba Pura, South Bali
Tel: 0361-770-300**

Are you good at sneaking up on people? Do you like crawling along the ground and hiding behind trees? Are you aged 11 or over? If you've answered 'yes' to all the above, then paintballing might be your thing! Paintball Bali will provide you with all the equipment you need, including coveralls, paintball guns, and the paint pellets. If there are only a few of you, join forces with other vacationers and play with a larger group. Call ahead (preferably by a few days) to book.

Motion Indoor Skate Park
**Off Jl Sunset Road, Kuta
Tel: 081-236-490-555**

If you want to work on your board skills, but you've had enough of sun and surf, try skateboarding instead! This indoor skateboard park has been built by the owners of the Motion Skate School in Legian, and boasts several different ramps for beginners as well as those who are pro skaters. The entrance price only includes the helmet rental, but for a very reasonable fee you can rent a board too. To get there, go to Jl Sunset Road, and turn into an unpaved road between the Carrefour store and the gas station. The skatepark is in a large warehouse. Call for more details.

Canggu Club

Jl Pantai Berawa, Banjar Tegal Gundul, Canggu
Tel: 0361-844-6385

Feeling sporty? The Canggu Club has great facilities – large sports fields, a big pool as well as a kids' pool, tennis and squash courts – as well as a library and nice restaurants. The club caters mainly to locals and vacationers who are staying in villas in Seminyak to Canggu, but a little-known secret is that they also have day memberships – for a fee! Apart from the facilities, they also have great multi-sport activity days, and organize the occasional barbeque or dance night. Call for more details.

IT'S RAINING

A lot of outdoor activities can still be fun when it's raining, but if you want to stay dry, we've picked some interesting activities for you to consider. Don't forget, you don't have to wait for rain to enjoy the (mostly indoor) activities listed below!

Balinese Cultural Creation
Jl Pulau Alor Permai 88, Denpasar
Tel: 0361-747-2556 / 0361-968-4903
The whole family can have lessons together at this center. They teach all sorts of Balinese arts and crafts, but they particularly recommend the kite painting, gamelan playing, batik making and Balinese dancing, for kids. They don't have lessons timetabled, but they're happy to arrange them to fit your schedule. Call for more details.

Museum Puri Lukisan
Jl Raya Ubud, Ubud
Tel: 0361-971 159 /
0361-975-136
This museum which houses traditional art such as wood carvings and paintings, also runs workshops for kids to learn all sorts of skills such as mask painting, Balinese dance, *gamelan* playing, batik, traditional painting, kite making, basketry and beading. Open 8am–4pm, except on Balinese holidays. Please call for more details on times and prices.

Pondok Pekak Library & Resource Center
Monkey Forest Road, Ubud
Tel: 0361-976-194
The Pondok library, which is next to the Ubud football field, is stocked with lots

IT'S POURING

of English and Indonesian books for both adults and children. But that's not all – they also run workshops for tourists on Balinese painting, dance etc, as well as the occasional reading or talk. Please call for more details.

Paon Bali Cooking Class
Laplapan Village, Ubud
Tel: 081-337-939-095

Visit a market and learn about ingredients, before being taken to a traditional village in Ubud. As an added extra, you'll learn all about village life from your knowledgeable guide as he drives! Once there, the Balinese chef will demonstrate several yummy dishes (with a little help from participants), which you can eat afterwards. Please call to discuss menus and details. They can pick you up from anywhere in Bali – but the pick-up is only free from within Ubud.

Jenggala Keramik Paint-a-Pot
Jl Uluwatu II, Jimbaran
Tel: 0361-703-311

If you've still got a few days left before you leave Bali, and want to make a unique souvenir, then this place is for you! The workshop stocks a range of white ceramic items – plates, bowls, mugs etc. Choose your favorite piece and plan your masterpiece ... then get painting. Everyone old enough to hold a paintbrush can take part, but if your parents prefer to shop or relax while you paint, there's a shop full of beautiful tableware, pottery making demonstrations and a nice café to keep them happy. Your ceramic creation needs to be fired (baked) in a kiln, to 'fix' the glaze so you won't be able to take it home right away – it can be collected 2–4 days later. Call for more details.

IT'S RAINING,

MOVIES

There are two regular cinemas in Bali – the **Galeria Cineplex 21** (Bali Galeria Mall, Simpang Siur, Kuta, tel: 0361-767-021) which caters to foreigners with English-language movies, and the **Wisata Cineplex 21**, in Denpasar (3/F, Pertokoan Lokitasari, Tel: 0361-423-023). The Wisata plays mainly Indonesian movies. Call for more details on movies and showtimes. Whichever cinema you choose to go to, check to make sure the movie you want to see hasn't been dubbed into Indonesian!

There is also an open-air screen at the **Ciak Cine Bar** restaurant – see pg 39 for details.

INDOOR FUN

Bali Fun World
Jl Lettu, 1 Wayan Sutha 11,
Banjar Peninjoan, Batuan, Sukawati
Tel: 0361-294-924
This indoor playground has something for every age – there's a special area for kids aged 6 and below, which has some mini slides, a soft climbing area, as well as bouncy castles, a ball pit, trampoline, playhouse and much, much more. Older kids (and fun-loving parents) can whoop it up on the rodeo bull ride, or the bungee trampolines. There are also huge slides, a climbing wall, basketball hoops, a games room stocked with PS2 and PS3, and more.

One of the oddest attractions at Bali Fun World is the Sumo wrestling game. The rules are simple: you and your opponent climb into a plastic 'body' suit, which is inflated until you are as huge as a Sumo wrestler, and then you try to knock each other over! If your parents get tired and need to rest, send them to the cafe – there is a good supply of newspapers and magazines provided, as well as free coffee/tea and WiFi. Open Tues–Fri 9.30am–9pm, and from 9am–9pm on the weekend.
Closed on Monday.

IT'S POURING

Tenpin Bowling at the Bowling Center, Kuta Paradiso Hotel

Jl Kartika Plaza, Tuban, Kuta
Tel: 0361-761-414

Challenge your family to a bowling game – and see how many strikes you can pick up in this modern 18-lane bowling alley in the heart of Kuta.

TimeZone – video games arcade

We wouldn't normally recommend you travel to an island paradise then spend time playing video-arcade games; but if it's raining and your mother is in full-on shopping mode, you might like to know that there are some TimeZone Game Arcades you can escape into! You'll find one on the top floor of the **Matahari Kuta Square** department store in Kuta, and on the ground floor of the **Matahari Center**, Legian (both pg 34).

SHOP TILL YO

There are tons of shops, street stalls and markets in Bali — ask your hotel to recommend a good shopping street. We like Jl Padma and the market on Jl Melasti in Legian; Jl Legian in Kuta; and the big tourist market at the corner of Jl Raya Ubud and Jl Monkey Forest Road in Ubud. Bargaining is expected in most places, but remember to always be polite and smile while you bargain!

Kartika Discovery Mall

Located opposite the **Waterbom** park, this mall has over 95 shops and two department stores. In addition to the usual brands, you will also find a large handicraft shop and **Kids Station** (for games and toys). There are also several restaurants and cafés.

Matahari Kuta Square

Jl Bakung Sari 1, Kuta
Tel: 0361-757-588

This department store is located in Kuta Square – a street packed with shops selling both real and fake designer goods. If your mother thinks things are too cheap to be real, they're probably fake! Inside the Matahari however, most things, although reasonably priced, are genuine. Look for local handicrafts on the ground floor or visit the top-floor kids' department (**TimeZone Games Arcade**, see pg 33).

Bali Galeria Mall

Simpang Siur, Kuta

Along with the usual selection of shops and a food hall, this mall contains the **Galeria 21 Cineplex** where reluctant shoppers can watch a movie while the shopaholics hit the shops!

u DROP

Matahari Center
Jl Legian 117, Legian
This Matahari department store is similar to the one in Kuta Square. The **TimeZone** is on the ground floor.

Geneva Handicraft Center
Jl Raya Kerobokan 100, Seminyak
The prices are fixed (no bargaining) in this huge warehouse packed with Indonesian handicrafts, but you're likely to find great bargains here, anyway!

Hardy's Sanur
Jl Danau Tamblingan 136, Sanur
This huge supermarket is stocked with reasonably priced souvenirs and handicrafts on the 2nd and 3rd floors. Similar to the sister store in Nusa Dua. Bargaining is expected!

SPECIALIST SHOPS

Enchanted Books
Jl Raya Kerobokan 69, Seminyak
Tel: 0361-734-822
This bookshop also stocks a range of games and all sorts of toys.

Monkey Monkey
Jl Monkey Forest, Ubud
Tel: 081-2364-451
This is a great shop to buy gifts, as it stocks all sorts of things – toys, clothes, photo frames, wind chimes, cushions, bags, jewelry, fridge magnets – all with a monkey theme!

FOOD, GLOR

Biku
Jl Petitenget 888, Seminyak
Tel: 0361-857-0888
This charming and quirky little restaurant with a
bookshop serves everything from breakfast to dinner,
and we recommend it for high tea. Creative sandwiches,
delicious cakes and nibbles are served alongside
scones with jam and cream. Kids can order their own
high tea – with mini teapots and fairy cakes!

Ku De Ta
Jl Kayu Aya 9, Seminyak. Tel: 0361-736-969
People flock to this trendy restaurant to see and be
seen! The prices are high for Bali and the food is just
okay, but it makes up for all that with the atmosphere
– relaxed with comfy daybeds, right on the beach and
wonderful view. If your parents need a treat, take them
in the late afternoon and let them lounge on a daybed,
while you dance in the garden to the music. Call and
ask about their Sunday 'Family Dayze' when there's a
bouncy castle and creative activities, or you can splash
about in the wading pool and play mini-golf. Eat to your
heart's content from the BBQ or the kids' menu.

La Lucciola
Jl Kayu Aya (next to Pura Petitenget – pg 14),
Seminyak. Tel: 0361-730-838
Popular with families because of the grassy
garden next to the beach, this Italian restaurant
is a favorite for Sunday brunch. Sit upstairs and enjoy
the ocean breeze! For dinner, go super early
and sit by the lawn.

Ristorante Italia
Hotel Kumala Pantai,
Jl Werkudara, Legian Kaja
Tel: 0361-755-500
The Ristorante is a little more
expensive than the Warung
Italia (pg 38), but it has a great

Balinese delights

Whatever you want to eat, it's likely that you can get it in Bali. But don't just eat burgers – try some Balinese food too. Some good examples are sate lilit (minced seafood or meat mixed with herbs and spices, wrapped around a skewer and grilled), babi guling (roasted suckling pig), bebek/ayam betutu (stuffed duck or chicken wrapped in banana leaves, then cooked till tender) and babi kecap (pork stewed in a delicious sweet soy sauce). Other Indonesian dishes to try are nasi goreng (fried rice) or lumpia (deep-fried spring roll). Most Indonesian food isn't spicy – but watch out for the sauces (sambals) as they can set your mouth on fire!

beachside location, and an air-conditioned area for when it's really hot! The homemade gnocchi, pizza and gelato (apparently the chocolate is heavenly) come recommended.

Ryoshi

Jl Raya Seminyak 17, Seminyak
Tel: 0361-731-152

This chain of Japanese restaurants is very popular and can also be found in Kuta, Ubud, Nusa Dua and Sanur – but locals say this branch is the best. Excellent fresh sushi and all the usual favorites too. It's not fancy, or expensive, but the fact that it is so popular is proof that the food is good!

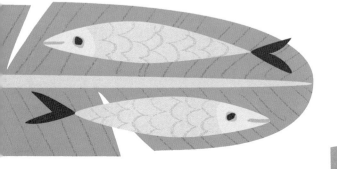

Sarong
Jl Petitenget 19x, Kerobokan, Kuta
Tel: 0361-737-809

Can a posh, ultra-groovy restaurant also be family friendly? Yes! Anyone with adventurous taste buds will like this relaxed restaurant and love the food – which is Asian with a twist. The curries are particularly yummy, and the bartender will make you a great fruity drink!

Warung Italia
Jl Kunti 2, Seminyak. Tel: 0361-737-437

This relaxed little restaurant is owned and run by an Italian native – and it shows in the food! It's famed for delicious pastas, crispy pizzas baked in a wood-fired oven, as well as the buffet of daily specials and yummy desserts. It's also very reasonably priced, and popular – get there early to grab seats. It has a newer, sister restaurant in Legian.

Warung Made
Jl Raya Seminyak, Seminyak
Tel: 0361-732-130

Like its sister restaurant in Kuta (on Jl Pantai Kuta), you can eat both international and Balinese dishes (though insiders say the curries are the best!) at this casual restaurant. The Seminyak branch has a nice garden, or you can sit indoors at the *warung*-style tables i.e. long tables that many people can share.

Zanzibar
(Blue Ocean/Double Six Beach)
Jl Double Six, Legian. Tel: 0361-733-529

Sit inside or outside to enjoy the Mediterranean-inspired food (or burgers/fish and chips if you prefer). The breakfast and lunch menus are simple, but there is a larger selection for dinner. It's not gourmet, but the setting is lovely. The roof terrace has a good view of the firedancers and drummers who often perform on the beach.

OUS FOOD

CANGGU & KEROBOKAN

The Beach House Restaurant (Echo Beach)

Jalan Pura Batu Mejan, Canggu. Tel: 0361-747-4604

This relaxed, reasonably priced restaurant is popular with families and can get crowded at times. But if you're nearby, it's worth a visit. The surfside position means that kids can enjoy the beach, or watch the surfers (swimming is not recommended as the waves can get very rough). They're open all day and there is a choice of dishes from all over the world. If you want to have the evening BBQ buffet, get there at least an hour before sunset to beat the rush. On Sunday evenings, there is often live music playing.

Ciak Cine Bar

**Jl Gunung Salak 44, Kerobokan
Tel: 0361-789-2804**

Feast on Italian food, then relax on a mattress in front of the open-air screen and watch a movie! Occasionally, they arrange 'party nights' for teens, where you can dance the night away or sing karaoke. Call for details on films and show times.

Om Organic Restaurant

**Jl Batu Bolong, Canggu Beach
Tel: 0361-960-4121**

Have a yummy organic meal in a house made out of bamboo! There are many tempting things on both the adults' and kids' menus (samosas, quesadilla, pastas, as well as other delicious meat, fish and vegetarian dishes). Save room for chocolate mousse or the apple crumble with ice cream. On the weekends, they serve breakfast too. There's even a playroom with toys for your younger sister or brother ... or you!

39

Sate Bali
Jl Laksmana 22a, Kerobokan
Tel: 0361-736-734
Can you guess what the speciality of this small and
reasonably priced place is? Yup, sate! All sorts of meat
and seafood *sate* chargrilled to perfection. If you're
hungry, have the *rijsttafel* – it's fun to share. *Rijsttafel* is
a Dutch word meaning 'rice table'. It's a feast of rice and
lots of different small dishes ... yum!

JIMBARAN BAY

Lia Café
Jl Pantai Kedonganan, Jimbaran Bay
Tel: 081-2390-7411
There are dozens of seafood restaurants on
Jimbaran Beach, but beware – some have been
known to cheat tourists and charge them
too much for their seafood! You won't
have that problem at Lia, which is one
of the oldest restaurants on the beach.
Sit with the sand between your toes
and enjoy delicious seafood, which
has been marinated and barbequed.
To find Lia, go to the beach end of
Jl Pemelisan Agung, where it meets
Jl Pantai Kedonganan – near Hotel
Keraton. Facing the beach, turn left. It
is near the end of the row of seafood
restaurants. Open 9am–midnight.

NUSA DUA &
TANJUNG BENOA

Boneka Restaurant –
St Regis Bali Resort
Kawasan Pariwisata, Nusa Dua Lot S6,
Nusa Dua
Tel: 0361-8478-111
If you wake up hungry on Sunday, head to the St Regis

Hotel. The Boneka is famous for its Sunday brunch buffet, which features yummy smoothies and a variety of food from around the world. There's also a children's corner with toys and popcorn, where your little sister or brother (or even you) can hang out while your parents relax and enjoy the live music. It's not cheap, but it has the reputation of being very good.

Bumbu Bali
Jl Pratama, Tanjung Benoa
Tel: 0361-774-502
This is one of Bali's best-known restaurants – if you eat here you enjoy real, traditional Balinese food. Order the *rijsttafel* to try a selection of dishes. Open noon–11pm daily. There are often Balinese dance performances on Friday evenings, and the chef also occasionally runs cooking classes.

Nusa Dua Beach Grill
Pantai Geger (Geger Beach)
Tel: 0361-7434-779
Enjoy the ocean breeze and watch the seaweed harvesters as you drink the delicious fruity smoothies, and eat yummy pizzas, pastas, salads or fresh seafood (including fish and chips!). There's a sign on the wall that says 'clothing optional' which tells you how laid-back the place is. It's a lovely relaxing spot to spend a sunny afternoon, as is Geger Beach itself, with its gentle waves and tide pools.

SANUR

Café Batujimbar
Jl Danau Tamblingan 75a, Sanur
Tel: 0361-287-374
Sit inside or out to enjoy the delicious breakfast (the banana and blueberry pancakes are amazing), lunch or dinner; both Indonesian and Western dishes. Or, drop by for a refreshing fruit juice or smoothie and a brownie! Open 8.30am–11pm.

FOOD, GLOR

Fortune Cookie
Jl Sudamala 5, Sanur
Tel: 0361-283-342

This small Chinese restaurant is popular with families – the food is yummy and MSG free. The dumplings and crispy butterfly fish are recommended. Save room for the fortune cookie! Open for lunch and dinner.

Kayu Manis Café
Jl Tandakan 6, Shindu, Sanur
Tel: 0361-289-410

This cozy little restaurant seats only 18 people – and because the food is good, it's always full. If you want to try their food (a mixture of Western and Eastern-inspired dishes), make sure you go early or book!

UBUD

Café Wayan Ubud
Jl Monkey Forest, Ubud
Tel: 0361-975-447

This café started life as a little food stall. The fact that it's now a big restaurant, says a lot about the food. It's open from breakfast to dinner, and serves food from all over the world – though their Balinese dishes are recommended. The chocolate cake is famous! Sit indoors, or outside in a lovely garden.

Fly Café
Jl Raya, Lungsiakan, Ubud
Tel: 0361-975-440

This laid back, open style café is a favorite with the expats – because the food is good, and cheap. Try the meaty ribs in sticky sauce and follow it up with the key lime pie for dessert!

Ibu Oka
Jl Suweta, Tegal Sari 2, Ubud
Tel: 0361-976-345

This tiny roadside restaurant is far from fancy – but it's been voted as the place with the best *babi guling* (roast suckling pig). Have the tender pork and crispy skin on coconut flavored rice – but unless you are a big chili fan, ask them to hold back on the red *sambal* sauce – it's really spicy! Only open for lunch – go early, as the pork often runs out about 2pm.

Kafe Batan Waru
Jl Dewi Sita, Ubud
Tel: 0361-977-528
Any time you're hungry, you can eat well at this casual restaurant – they open for breakfast, lunch and dinner (sandwiches, pasta, or Balinese food). The desserts are yummy too – choose from apple crumble, cheesecake or a melt-in-the-mouth chocolate tart! Open 8.30am–midnight. (There's a branch in Kuta too – near the Waterbom park.)

Mumbul Restaurant and Bar
Jl Raya Ubud, Ubud
Tel: 0361-975-364
Known for its fabulous ice creams, you can also enjoy homemade pasta and a good variety of Balinese and Western food. There's a nice terrace overlooking the river.

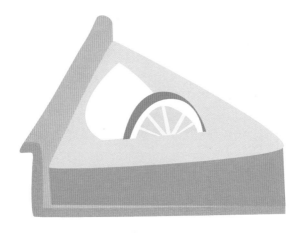

BALI KNOW-

FAST FACTS

- Bali is one of the 17,508 islands of Indonesia. The official language is Bahasa Indonesia, but many people also speak Bahasa Bali (a language which is only spoken, not written!) as well as English and other local dialects.

- The currency of Bali is the Indonesian rupiah. Price tags often have huge numbers on them, but 9,000 rupiah is worth approximately 1 US dollar, so things are not quite as expensive as they seem at first look!

- As Bali is close to the equator, the temperature doesn't vary much – it's hot all year round! There is a rainy season though – between October and March – when it can rain heavily, especially in the afternoon. But it doesn't usually rain all day, so you can still have fun in the sun!

- The population of Bali is more than 3.5 million. Most people are Hindus here, which is unusual, as the rest of Indonesia is largely Muslim.

- Bali's capital city is called Denpasar. The government is based there, and it's a good place to go shopping, but it doesn't have many tourist attractions.

T-ALL

DOS AND DON'TS

- **Do** drink lots of water (but only the bottled kind).

- **Do** show respect when visiting a temple – wear modest clothes and put a sarong on.

- **Do** be careful not to step on the small offerings (for the gods) you see on the street.

- **Do** bargain when you're shopping – but remember to be pleasant and smile a lot!

- **Do** be mindful of your belongings – especially when there are monkeys around. They are very good at grabbing anything loose and shiny!

- **Do** relax and prepare to wait – the Balinese follow a gentle pace of life, and things may take a little longer than at home.

- **Don't** go out without wearing sunscreen, a hat and insect repellent!

- **Don't** take or give things using your left hand – that hand is considered to be 'unclean'.

- **Don't** touch anyone on the head – the head is thought to be where one's soul lives.

- **Don't** touch people with your feet or point your feet toward anyone's head. Pointing your finger at people is considered impolite too.

- **Don't** go near the monkeys or stray dogs – they may bite! They usually won't come near if you don't approach or show you have food.

BALI KNOW-

SPEAK THE LINGO

Bahasa Bali is difficult to learn, as there are many 'levels' of politeness – what you'd say to a friend is different to what you'd say to a teacher. So, here we are going to teach you Bahasa Indonesia. The Indonesian words below are written as they are pronounced, rather than how they are normally spelled – e.g. 'sla-mat' is actually written as 'selamat'. Indonesians roll the letter 'r' like the French do, so if you see an 'r', try rolling it.

- **Good morning :** sla-mat pah-gee

- **Good day (around 11am-3pm) :** sla-mat see-ang

- **Good afternoon (3pm till sunset) :** sla-mat sor-reh

- **Good evening :** sla-mat ma-lum

- **Good bye (only use when you are the person leaving) :** sla-mat ting-gul

- **My name is... :** nam-ma say-ya...

- **Thank you :** tree-ma kah-seeh

- **I'm sorry :** ma-af

- **Delicious! :** eh-nak!

- **How much is this? :** berap-pa har-gan-ya ini?

- **I don't understand :** saya tid-deh mon-gart-ti

- **Do you speak English? :** be-sa be-chara bah-sa in-gris?

- **Where is the rest room please? :** dee mana kam-ma ke-chil?

- **Yes :** ya   **No :** ti-dak

- **Bottled Water :** ai-yurr bo-toll

T-ALL

BALI TRIVIA

Bali has a couple of active volcanoes, the highest of which is called Gunung Agung. The most active volcano in Bali is called Gunung Batur; it last erupted in 2000.

Nyepi (Hindu New Year) is known as the 'Day of Silence', when all of Bali shuts down. The exact date varies, at it's based on the lunar calendar. People spend the day in silence, and don't use any electrical items. They aren't even supposed to turn on the lights or light fires. Everything is closed and tourists are expected to stay in their hotels. The night before Nyepi is very different – religious ceremonies and parades take place in every village. Locals set off firecrackers and bang drums to scare away bad luck and demons!

Ubud gets its name from the ancient Balinese word *ubad*, which means 'healing'. It's thought that a few hundred years ago, Ubud was the place people went for cures when they were ill.

If you visit a temple, you will probably see pagoda-like shrines with multi-tiered roofs. These shrines are known as *meru* – after Mount Meru, which is believed to be the home of the gods.

A popular form of transportation in Bali is a little bus called a *bemo*. It has no meter though, so passengers have to bargain before they set off.

The double-weave ikat cloth made in the village of Tenganan is so time consuming to make that a craftsman can take years to finish one piece! Because of this, and the belief that it protects the wearer from bad luck, it is very expensive.

You won't find beef on a traditional Balinese menu, because most Balinese are Hindus. The Hindus regard the cow as sacred, and don't eat beef.

Gigantic komodo dragons are native to Indonesia, though not to Bali. Adult dragons grow to 3 meters / 10 feet long and can weigh almost as much as your dad! They only need to eat about once a month, but each meal can weigh about three quarters of their own bodyweight!

◀ Write an interesting fact you find in here

Wayan is probably the most common name in Bali, as it is the name given to many first-born children – girls as well as boys. Second-born children are often called Made, the third Nyoman and the fourth Ketut ... and then the cycle starts again – with the fifth child being called Wayan!

T-ALL

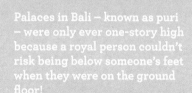

Palaces in Bali – known as puri – were only ever one-story high because a royal person couldn't risk being below someone's feet when they were on the ground floor!

In Bali there is a measurement of time called akejepan Barong – which means 'a Barong's wink'. As the Barong mask never winks, this is the same as saying: 'not in a very very very long time (if ever)'!

MAKE A NOTE

Make a note of your best Bali memories and experiences right here!

_____

_____

_____

_____

_____

_____

_____

_____

_____

_____

_____

WEIRD & WONDERFUL

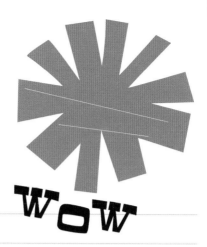

WOW

KEEPSAKES

Draw and stick pictures or tickets here!

fun!

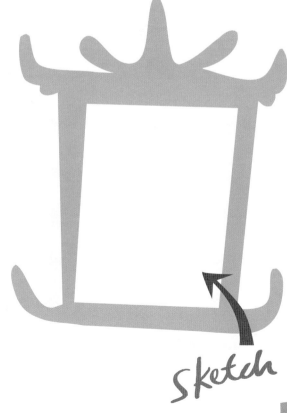

sketch

EXPLORE UBUD

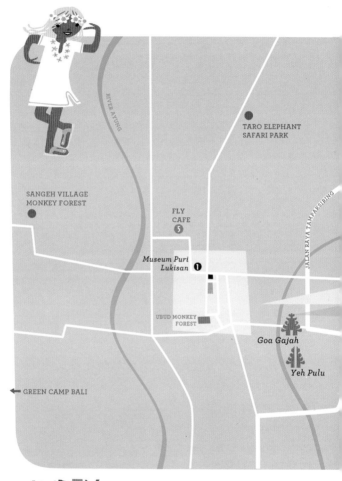

TARO ELEPHANT SAFARI PARK

RIVER AYUNG

SANGEH VILLAGE MONKEY FOREST

FLY CAFE ⑤

JALAN RAYA TAMPAKSIRING

Museum Puri Lukisan ❶

UBUD MONKEY FOREST

Goa Gajah

Yeh Pulu

← GREEN CAMP BALI

INDEX

Eating

Shopping

● Nearby attractions

Bali is not huge, so you can still enjoy both beach and inland attractions even if you prefer to stay in one place. But since some of the listed attractions are more easily reached from Ubud, we've included a more detailed map of the area, so you can plan your visit better!

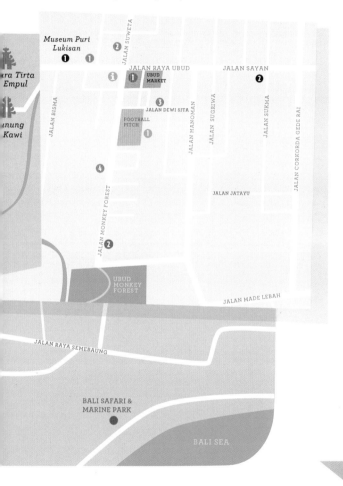

INDEX

UBUD
see map
on p54

UBUD
see p54